Foxes, Mostly

Judy Edmonds

Published by Judy Peters, 2023.

While every precaution has been taken in the preparation of this book, the publisher assumes no responsibility for errors or omissions, or for damages resulting from the use of the information contained herein.

FOXES, MOSTLY

First edition. October 22, 2023.

ISBN: 979-8223221982

Written by Judy Edmonds.

Table of Contents

To Graham. Blame him.

In the cold

In winter's chill the world turns cold.
As snowflakes fall a tale unfolds.
The air is crisp with frosty bite
As daylight fades into the night.
The trees stand bare, their branches stark.
In winter's hush they leave their mark.
A blanket of snow pure and white
Covers the earth in soft moonlight.
Footprints crunch in the frozen ground.
By the fireside we find our retreat
In cosy warmth and tales so sweet.
With playful words we are beguiled
As winter's magic is reconciled
And snowflakes fall and icicles strike.

Beneath the shadowed urban sprawl

Beneath the shadowed urban sprawl
Where the mundane lives, its ethos small,
Exist elusive foxes wild and bright
In the depth's of city's endless light
Their fur a rusty copper hue.
Like whispered dreams both old and new
In solitude they tread the streets.
Masters of secrets, their presence discreet
In night's embrace they dance and play,
Their cunning minds at work, they sway
Through alleys, parks and garden gates.
They navigate as if helped by fates
In concrete jungles they find their way
Adapting, thriving, come what may.
Their eyes, like amber jewels, do gleam
In this modern cityscape of dreams.
Though life's harshness surrounds them, stark,
Magical foxes, they leave a mark,
A reminder of nature's enduring grace
In our urban world, an enchanted place.

Or so it seems...

In moonlit woods where secrets hide
There roam the foxes, sleek and sly,
Their coats of silver, eyes of fire,
In twilight's hush, they never tire.
Magical beings of ancient lore
They dance through shadows forever more.
Their tails aglow with mystic light
Guiding lost souls through the night.
Invisible threads of fate they weave
In realms where people scarcely believe
They whisper secrets to the breeze
And share with the moon their tales of ease.
Through silent incantations they speak
In language that stars and spirits seek.
With cunning smiles, they cast their spells
Invisible as dreams in hidden dells.
These magical foxes, guardians of the night,
Invisible wonders. In the pale moonlight
They guard the realms where magic thrives,
In the hearts of dreamers where hope survives.
So heed the call of the foxes' song
In moonlit woods where they belong.
For in their world of mystery and dreams

You'll find the magic ...
Or so it seems...

Fire wolves

Fire wolves, a spectre in night's ballet they convey.
Their flames ignite like a fervent romance.
In the city of shadows they boldly advance.
In cobblestone alleys where love's secrets reside
Fire wolves dance, passion unable to hide.
Their eyes, burning embers, let tales unfold,
In verses of longing, their desires unfold.
Amidst smoky cafes and whispered desire
They prowl, a symbol of love's untamed fires.
Their howls, like jazz notes, drift through the air
In the heart of the city, where nothing is fair.
With a flick of their tails sparks of rebellion ignite,
In the world of the spirits where day turns to night.
In this existential reverie they take their stance
Fire wolves of ardour in a mystic romance.
They can make us believe in love's fiery essence
Where dreams cannot deceive

Future foxes

In the realm of ethereal pixilations
Foxes blaze with cyber incarnations
Mechanical tails, electric fire
In the futurist night, they transpire
Bolts of lightening through circuit veins
In their code, a world unchains
Stealth and speed in bytes and sparks
In digital landscapes they embark
Pixel-foxes, neon dreams
Silicon realms and quantum streams
Binary hearts in silicon chests
Cyberpunk spirit put to the test
Through the cables they swiftly dart
Masters of the electric art
In the futurist dance they immerse
Magic and machines in the universe
Their data tails leave traces bright
In the neon maze of byte and byte
Foxes of the future, they roam free
In the digital realm, where dreams can be

Fox wedding

In a meadow bathed in twilight's tender glow
Where ancient oaks whispered secrets low
Amidst the dappled moonlight's gentle sway
A fox wedding unfolds in the soft night's display.
Their pelts adorned with nature's grace,
Two foxes meet in this sacred space,
With eyes that gleam like starlit skies
They exchange vows within celestial ties.
In a union of love, they stand so near,
Their hearts, like wild rivers, free and clear.
Their vows, a chorus in nature's choir
As they pledge their love by the woodland fire.
Beneath the silvered canopy of leaves above.
To the meadows' whispers and the breeze's song
They dance as one where they both belong

In this moonlight meadow, under the starry dome
Their union is etched in the heart of home.

Maiden mother crone

In twilight's gentle, fading light
Three phases of a wondrous sight.
Woman, Mother, Crone divine
Their essence in this verse entwined.
The Woman, young and full of grace
With laughter in her sparkling grace
Her heart a garden, blooming free
A beacon of vitality.
The Mother, strong and deeply wise
With love that never truly dies
Her arms embrace
Her warmth does show
A nurturing, eternal flow.
The Crone, in wisdom's silver shroud
With eyes that have seen life's ebb and crowd
Her spirit aged yet still so strong
A well of ancient, timeless song.
Three aspects of the feminine soul
In harmony their stories told.
From youth to age, they beautifully spin
The tale of life where we all begin.
Oh, Woman, Mother, Crone, appear,
In your presence, we find what's clear,

The cycles of life, the eternal dance,
In your embrace, we find our chance

Nadja's foxes

In twilight's surrealist dreamscape they tread,
Foxes of enchantment, ethereal thread,
Their tales a swirl of opalescent hues,
In the realm of dreams, where mystery accrues.
Eyes aglow like midnight stars in the void,
They weave illusions, by reality destroyed.
Through strange warped landscapes they elegantly glide,
Where logic and reasons in shadows hide.
Their paws, a brush to paint the canvas strange,
In landscapes abstract, where colours rearrange.
Foxes of magic, mystical and untamed,
In dreams' distorted mirrors, they're named,
In dreams and waking, realms intertwine,
Foxes of wonder, the boundary redefine.
Half-seen spectres in the maze of night,
Guiding us through visions with shimmering light.
Oh, magical foxes, moonlight and rare,
In the subconscious realm we find you there.
A dreamlike dance in the poet's embrace,
Surrealist foxes, in beauty and grace.

Dire wolves

In shadows dark and cloaked with dread
Dire wolves roam, their eyes blood-red.
Their fur, a tempest's swirling shroud.
With fangs that gleam like blades of doom
They haunt the night in the Stygian gloom,
Their howls a dirge, a mournful cry,
Infernal creatures under a starry sky.
In the abyss of their obsidian gaze
The depths of Hades, a fiery maze.
They tread the path of the fallen souls.
With every step they stoke the pyre,
In their wake, the world's set afire.
As harbingers of doom they are crowned where darkness is bound.
In the style of dread they prowl and they creep,
Infernal guardians of the abyss so deep.

Always was

In the heart of distant lands, so vast,
Where gumtrees sway and deserts contrast,
With foreign eyes we'll try to trace
The essence of the bush's grace.
With eucalypt leaves that shimmer high
Beneath the endless Southern sky.
In the bush's heart, the wilds persist.
Arid plains, red earth so wide,
In summer's heat where creatures hide,
Yet life persists, resilient and tough.
The kookaburra's laughter rings
As the bushland's ancient rhythm sings,
In nature's verses, strong and free,
The Australian bush for all to see.
Where nature's beauty takes its stand.

Urban jungle

In the urban jungle where the neon lights gleam
Dwell the foxes as in shadows they scheme.

Their coats, mottled grey with hints of rust.

In the city's maze they place their truth.
With eyes that flicker like a city's heartbeat

They prowl through alleyways, their steps discreet.

In the shadows they are elusive and sly,
Navigating chaos as the night drifts by.

Their tales like whispers of forgotten tales.

In the metropolitan rhythm their mystery trails.
Amidst the concrete canyons they wend their way.

Urban foxes at night time, they find their way.

In the city's midst, where life and dreams entwine,
Urban foxes, in their elusiveness, define.

In the pulse of the city, where stories ignite,
Urban foxes dance in the poet's moonlight.

Mrs Ramsay – my doppelganger

Mrs Ramsay's ghost, a spectre of grace and melancholy,
Drifts through the recesses of my thoughts like a wispy shadow.
She lingers in the corners of my mind
Her presence both ethereal and haunting

Like the soft echo of a forgotten lullaby.

It's as if her essence has transcended time
Lingering in the intricate patterns of thought
Just as she once left an indelible mark on the lives she touched.
I see her in the shimmering waves of memory

A figure poised and regal

Presiding over the summer house with an air of elegance that defies the chaos of existence.
Her laughter like a delicate breeze still rustles the leaves of the old oak tree,
While her gaze, with its quiet understanding,
Seems to penetrate the depths of human experience.
Her spirit like a beacon guides us through the tumultuous seas of emotion,
Offering solace in times of despair and a proud sense of interconnectedness with the world around us.

Mrs Ramsay's ghost is a reminder that even in the vast expense of time certain souls endure,

Their presence woven into the very fabric of our thoughts and feelings.

The swirling crew

In the quiet meadow's gentle hush
Where foxes roam and rooks do rush,
It is easy to find one's muse
And in nature's rhythms enthuse.
Foxes with fur, auburn and sly,
Through the dappled woods they ply.
With grace and cunning they explore,
In twilight's embrace, they adore.
And rooks above, in ebony flight,
Caw and cackle in the fading light.
They dance in circles, a swirling crew.
In meadows and woods, they coexist
As if the poet's words are kissed.
Their tailss entwined with nature's grace
And in their place they find their place.

Azure dreams

Blue foxes in azure dreams are
A surreal sight, or so it may seem
As they take their flight, creatures of mystique
In the moon's soft light.
Their fur, a canvas of night's hues,
Echoes the navy sky, deep and true.
With eyes like sapphires they pierce the night
And gleam so bright.
Through moonlight meadows they gracefully glide
And to the poet's eyes they cannot hide
Their tales, like comets in the sky,
In the tapestry of dreams they mystify.
In the cobalt night their stories entwine
In a dance of magic where dreams align.
Blue foxes in poetic reverie, they thrive
In the heart of the night where dreams come alive.

Come skin-walk with me

Through the forest of future past
Kitsune longs to see
And walks out between two worlds
Come skin-walk with me.
In the autumn flames and trees
Kitsune longs for life
Within the rain of a fox wedding
Come skin-walk with me.

Spectral ballet, with foxes

In the twilight realm where enchantment takes flight
Magic foxes emerge from the depths of the night.
Their fur, a tapestry of moonbeam and shadow
They dance and weave with an eerie bravado.
With eyes like opals, they pierce through the dust.
They roam through alleys where secrets are sold
In the city's heart where mysteries unfold.
These cunning creatures, with sorcery entwined.
In the smoky haze of opium dreams they conjure illusions.
With tails like wisps of smoke, they enthrall.
Magic foxes, in the poet's phantasmagoria
Invoke the mystical, the surreal, the euphoria.
Their spectral ballet.

Feline zen

In the twilight's softest hush
A whiskered muse begins to blush.
As the poet with a playful pen
Weaves a world of feline zen
With tails that curl in whimsey's dance
They slink and prowl in moon's romance.
Each purring heart a hidden song
Weaves a world where all belong.
They saunter through the shadows deep
Where secrets in their silence keep,
With eyes like orbs so bright and wise,
In the deepest night their mystery lies.
In fur and furless, sleek and sly,
They make a world to soar and fly.
These feline souls, both wild and tame,
In poetic whispers stake their claim.

So, in this ode to cats we weave
A tapestry of tales.

Moonlight, moonlight, always moonlight

In moonlit woods where shadows softly fall,
There dwell the foxes, creatures of the night.
With fur aglow in silver's gentle light,
They weave enchantments beneath ancient thrall.
Their eyes, like stars, hold secrets yet untold,
Reflect the night, the cosmos in their gaze.
They move with grace through midnight's mystic haze.
In nature's dance, a tale of old unfolds.
With nimble feet, they tread on forest floors,
Their paws as silent as the whispered breeze.
In their presence, the ancient spirits tease,
As magical foxes roam these wooded shores.
Oh creatures rare, both cunning and beguiled.
In moonlit dreams, your legend is compiled.

FORME DEL MITO, ARNALDO POMODORO

It's three o'clock
should you be asleep?
Broken stars collide with bats
so much for sonar
Fruit bats don't need satellites
actually they do
No, not clouds
not rain
not fog
not plagues
The Milky Way has vanished
That can't be good
What is the morning?
the colour of twelve
the hunter's stew
The death mask four ways in a Brisbane square
The dog at the door and
the wolf at the fold
And the colour of twelve
and the water-rat drowning

Painted paws

In twilight's surrealist dreamscape they tread,
Foxes of enchantment, ethereal thread,
Their tales a swirl of opalescent hues,
In the realm of dreams, where mystery accrues.

Eyes aglow like midnight stars in the void,
They weave illusions, reality destroyed.
Through strange warped landscapes they elegantly glide,
Where logic and reasons in shadows hide.
Their paws, a brush to paint canvas strange,
In landscapes abstract, where colours arrange.
Foxes of magic, mystical and untamed,
In dreams' distorted mirrors, they're named,
In dreams and waking, realms intertwine,
Foxes of wonder, the boundary redefine.
Half-seen spectres in the labyrinth of night,
Guiding us through visions with shimmering light.
Oh, magical foxes, moonlit and rare,
In the subconscious realm we find you there.
A dreamlike dance in the poet's embrace,
Surrealist foxes, in beauty and grace.

A subject for me, in words to arrange

Foxes, magical,
Enigmatic and strange.
A subject for me,
In words to arrange.
Foxes, oh foxes,
What do we know?
Their tails in the grass,
They come and they go.
A fox is a fox is a fox,
Some would say,
But in their eyes,
Secrets gleam and sway.
Foxes, oh foxes,
So cunning and wise,
They wear a disguise,
A sly, foxy guise.
They trot through the woods,
In moonlight's gleam,
A dreamscape of shadow,
A fantastasical dream.
Their essence eludes,
Like words never found.
Their mysteries locked,

A riddle inside.
In the forest they play,
In realms undefined.
Magical foxes,
In enigma entwined.
Foxes, just foxes,
Or more profound?
In the endless repetition of their name,
Foxes, foxes, retain poetic flames.

Nocturnal ballet

In moon's pale shroud they converge,
Foxes and bats, creatures on't verge
Of night's inscrutable dance, they emerge,
Silent phantoms in twilight's serge.
Foxes with eyes aglow in the dark
Stealthy prowlers in the woodland's arc,
Their cunning minds an enigmatic spark,
Hunters of shadows in the stillness hark.
Bats with wings like whispers in flight,
Invisible threads weaving through the night,
Echoes in silence, their sonar's might,
Invisible worlds beyond human sight.
Together they roam, these twilight kin,
In a world of shadows, they begin
A nocturnal ballet, a dance of sin.
In the kingdom of night they reign within.

Two realms converge where darkness dwells
In the land of secrets where silence swells.
Foxes and bats, in their own spells,
In the mystic night their story tells.

Trickery a testament

In moonlight woods where secrets softly tread
There roam the foxes, magic in their eyes.
With coats of ember, tails a fiery thread,
They weave enchantments under starry skies.
In silver shadows, cunning is their grace.
They prance across realms where fantasy is real.
Their laughter echoes in the mystic space
Their trickery a testament to skill.
These creatures wise, from ancient tales of lore,
Hold secrets of the woods in whispered code.
With paws that paint the night upon the forest floor
They cast their spells where hidden wonder bode.
Magical foxes, guardians of the night,
In their enchantment, we may find pure delight.

Crimson secrets and enigmatic smiles

In the darkened woods where shadows grow
There lurks a secret who may only know?
Magical foxes, with eyes so deep,
In dreams and mysteries, their secrets keep.

Their fur, a tapestry of surreal designs,
In imagined landscapes, they intertwine,
With crimson secrets and enigmatic smiles
They walk the line where reality beguiles.
In twisted tales of suburban nights,
Where secrets hide in flickering lights,
These foxes roam in our minds,
In distorted landscapes, side by side
In dreams and nightmares they conspire
To set the world's logic on fire.
With coffee black as midnight's shroud
And owls that hoot both soft and loud,
Magical foxes in your gaze
Leave trails of mystery in their maze.
So in the twisted world that's spun
Where dreams and nightmares are as one
The magical foxes, sly and strange,
In our twisted imagination will always range.

Kitsune

In Japan, a fox known as Kitsune
With tricks and transformations does amuse
With nine tails she's sly
In folklore, oh my!
She's wily and clever, not to be confused!

A place where all things end

Amidst the shadowed canopy secrets whisper, concealed
In woodlands deep where ancient tales in branches are revealed.
The mournful sigh of ancient oaks,
Their wisdom etched in bark,
A symphony of rustling leaves, where time stands still, remark.
Beneath the shroud of twilight's veil elusive creatures roam,
Their eyes aglow in moonlight's gleam
They find their woodland home.
Mysteries woven in the mist, a labyrinth untold,
In tangled roots and mossy stones their secrets all unfold.
The scent of earth and damp decay
A scent of life anew.
Where fragile ferns and mushrooms thrive
In shades of green and blue.
A dance of dappled sunlight weaves through canopies of high.
In whispered vows the trees declare
Their branches touch the sky.
But lurking in this sylvan realm the darkness takes its toll,
As shadows cast by moonlight's grace, a haunting story to extol.

In this enigmatic woodlands' heart where dreams and nightmares blend,
Whose madness touches the mossy floor,

A place where all things end.

They chase the stars and paint the skies

Mystic foxes, they dance and prance.
In the moonlit night, they take a chance.
With fur so sleek and eyes that gleam
They rule the world of this magic dream.
They slink through shadows, silent as the breeze
Whispers of enchantment carried on the trees.
With tails that flicker, a spell they cast.
In their world the present and future merge fast.
They conjure moonbeams in their wake
Turn fallen leaves into wishes to make.
Their laughter echoes through the dark,
In their world there's no need for sparks.
These foxes are wild and untamed
With invisible boundaries they've never been maimed.
They chase the stars and paint the skies
In their magic world where dreams arise.
So let's raise a cheer for the magic they create.
These foxes of wonder, we celebrate,
In their secret world where dreams come alive
They teach us to believe and thrive.

With bramble and thorn

In the hidden hollows where secrets reside,
In the shadowed realms where the woodlands bide,
There dwell the hedge witches, wise and old.
With bramble and thorn they weave their spells
In the mossy glades where magic dwells,
Their cauldrons bubble with herbs and brews
In the heart of the forest where enchantment ensues.
Hedge witches, keepers of ancient lore,
In their hands nature's wisdom they implore
They whisper to the moon and converse with the trees.
Their spells are potions of love and desire,
In the quiet woods where the spirits conspire,
With incantations soft as the dark night's caress.

Summer playgrounds

Beneath the sun's warm golden glow
Where pink peppercorn trees do grow
In an old nostalgic dream
Old school playgrounds in the afternoon gleam.
With laughter echoing through the years
As children played, smothering fears,
The peppercorn trees in vibrant hues
Shaded games where friendships grew,
Their branches whispered secrets shared,
In the gentle breezes, some troubles bared.
The distinctive scent hung in the air.

Summer dreams

Among the garden's fragrant pose
Where roses bloom and swallow goes
In this quiet reflective rhyme
We find beauty woven through time.
Roses with petals soft and red
In gardens they raise their graceful heads.
Their perfume whispers secrets near.
And swallows with wings of blue and white
In flight they weave their daring flight
As in skies above they soar and play
And wistfully they find their way.
Together in harmony's gentle stream
With roses and swallows, my summer dream.

Realities collide

Beneath the brooding skies of yore
Where moors stretch wide and wild winds roar
A talking fox with fur of russet flame
Came whispering secrets, a creature untamed.
In the Heights where nature's might
Held sway over hearts, day and night,
This fox with eyes like fiery stars
Shared tales that reached from near to far.
With words that painted darkened moors,
A narrative woven in whispers and roars
The fox revealed hidden realms untold.
Through tempests and thunder it spoke with grace
In the timeless landscape, finding its place.
A guardian of secrets, a sage of the glen,
Through centuries past it whispered again and again.
A talking fox, a mystical guide
Through the poet's real, where realities collide.

Haiku

South Downs rolling high
Verdant hills touch endless sky
Nature's beauty nigh

Dartmoor's wild expanse
Moorland shrouded in mystic dance
Nature's ancient trance
Endless waves explore
Horizons' lapis width
Ocean's deep embrace

Don't miss out!

Visit the website below and you can sign up to receive emails whenever Judy Edmonds publishes a new book. There's no charge and no obligation.

https://books2read.com/r/B-A-KYCBB-BGTPC

BOOKS 2 READ

Connecting independent readers to independent writers.

About the Author

Judy Edmonds has studied history, librarianship, textile art and literature. One day she will embroider a story and index it. She is interested in the female gothic, specuative fiction and alternative history. Prose works are published under the name Judy Peters.

Read more at https://judy-peters.com.au/.

www.ingramcontent.com/pod-product-compliance
Lightning Source LLC
Chambersburg PA
CBHW071245130726
47998CB00003B/1063